WS

The Natural History Museum

Animal Close-Ups

Insects
and other minibeasts

Barbara Taylor

OXFORD
UNIVERSITY PRESS

OXFORD
UNIVERSITY PRESS

Great Clarendon Street, Oxford OX2 6DP

Oxford University Press is a department of the University of Oxford.
It furthers the University's objective of excellence in research, scholarship,
and education by publishing worldwide in

Oxford New York

Athens Auckland Bangkok Bogotá Buenos Aires
Cape Town Chennai Dar es Salaam Delhi Florence Hong Kong Istanbul
Karachi Kolkata Kuala Lumpur Madrid Melbourne Mexico City Mumbai
Nairobi Paris São Paulo Shanghai Singapore Taipei Tokyo Toronto Warsaw

with associated companies in Berlin Ibadan

Oxford is a registered trade mark of Oxford University Press
in the UK and in certain other countries

Text copyright © Barbara Taylor 2002
Photographs copyright © The Natural History Museum, London 2002
Photographs by Frank Greenaway

The moral rights of the author have been asserted

Database right Oxford University Press (maker)

First published 2002

British Library Cataloguing in Publication Data available

Paperback ISBN 0 19 910792 0

1 3 5 7 9 10 8 6 4 2

Printed in Hong Kong

Contents

About this book
This book takes a close look at insects, which
have six legs and three parts to their bodies.
It will also tell you about other minibeasts,
from spiders with eight legs to snails
with just one soft, squishy foot.

I am a beautiful butterfly.

I have four large wings and two long, thin antennae. I use my antennae for smelling things.

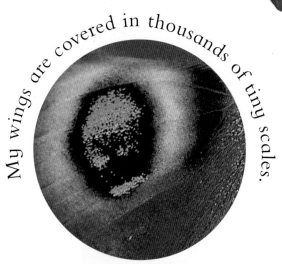

My wings are covered in thousands of tiny scales.

I am called a peacock butterfly because the pattern on my wings looks like the pattern on the feathers of a peacock.

6

When I hatched out of my egg, I was a hungry caterpillar.

My spikes helped to protect me from enemies.

Later, I changed into a pupa with thorny spines.

When I fold my wings together, you cannot see my bright colours. I can hide more easily like this.

After about two weeks, I pushed my way out of the pupa as a butterfly.

7

I am a speedy dragonfly.

I zoom around, scooping up flying insects with my long, spiny legs.

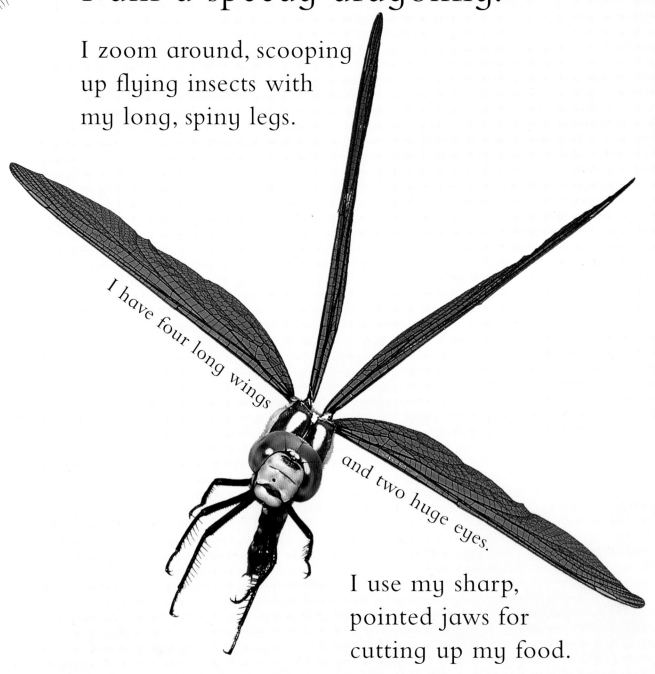

I have four long wings and two huge eyes.

I use my sharp, pointed jaws for cutting up my food.

8

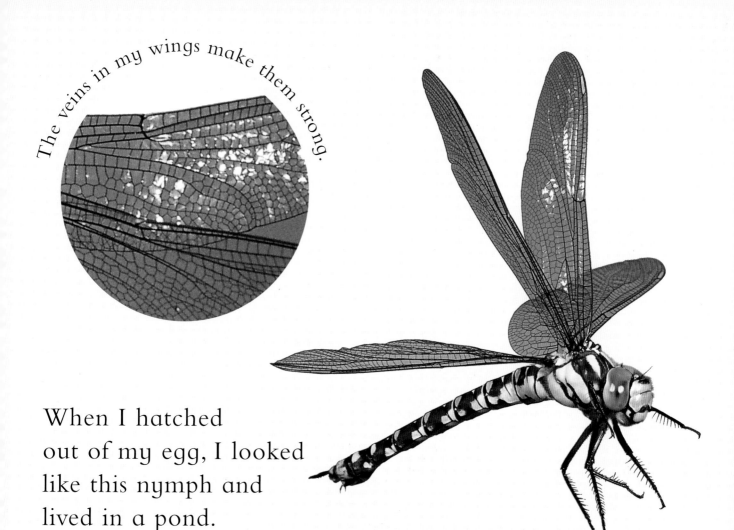

The veins in my wings make them strong.

When I hatched out of my egg, I looked like this nymph and lived in a pond.

When I grew up I changed into a dragonfly with wings. I can fly forwards, backwards, up and down, hover in one spot and stop suddenly.

9

I am a buzzy bumble bee.

My long, pointed tongue is like a straw. I use it to suck up the nectar from flowers. I make honey from nectar. I eat some of it and feed some to my young.

My long tongue sucks sweet nectar from flowers.

My wings fold over my back when I am not flying.

My six legs are divided into sections. I grip petals and leaves with hooks on the ends of my feet.

I collect pollen from flowers
and carry it in baskets on
my back legs. I take it to
my nest and feed
it to my young.

I feel and smell
things with these
bendy antennae.

I have two huge eyes
behind my antennae.

11

I am a stinging wasp.

My black and yellow stripes warn enemies that I am not good to eat. If they attack me, I might give them a nasty sting.

I am a queen wasp sleeping through the winter.

I have two antennae, two big eyes and biting mouthparts.

I cling on to plants using the claws on my legs.

12

I am a stripy wasp beetle.

My stripes make me look like a wasp, which warns my enemies to leave me alone. I only have stripes on my hard front wings. I hold them out stiffly while I fly with my thin back wings.

I tap my antennae like a real wasp as I scurry about. I have biting jaws.

My flying wings fold away neatly under my stripy wings.

13

I am a jumping cricket.

My enormous back legs
have strong muscles that help
me jump a long way. I have
a hard collar behind my head
that protects the front part
of my body.

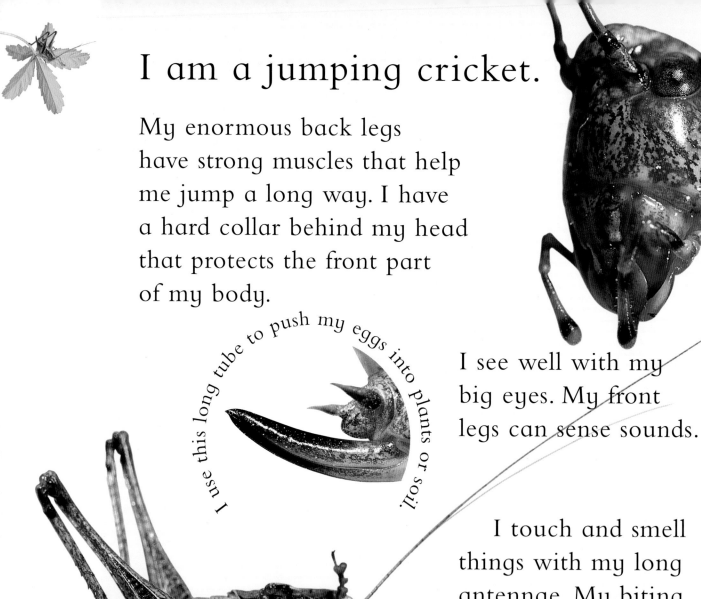

I use this long tube to push my eggs into plants or soil.

I see well with my
big eyes. My front
legs can sense sounds.

I touch and smell
things with my long
antennae. My biting
jaws cut and grind up
my food.

I am a creeping woodlouse.

I like to live in damp,
dark places and I eat
dead plants. I usually
come out at night.

My body has seven big segments and six smaller ones.

My two black eyes are on the sides of my head.

I have two large antennae
on my head. Under my
body I have fourteen
legs. I usually huddle
together with lots
of other woodlice.

15

I am a hairy tarantula.

I am a red-knee tarantula. I just fit into an adult's hand. I may look scary, but I am shy. My poisonous bite could hurt you, but not kill you. I can flick my prickly hairs at my enemies.

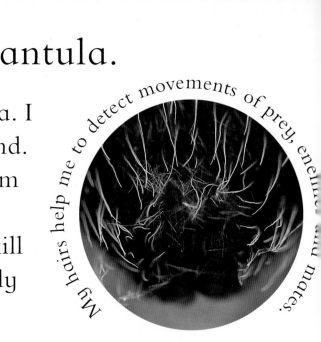

My hairs help me to detect movements of prey, enemies and mates.

I have eight legs, each
with seven parts. I
also have two palps
at the front of my body.
They look like short legs.
I use these to feel things
and to hold food.

I have eight eyes, but cannot see very far ahead.

The claws and hair tufts on my feet help me to cling on tight.

I am a scary scorpion.

I catch food with my big pincers.
I eat insects and spiders. I kill
my enemies with the sting
at the end of
my tail.

I have eight legs,
like a spider.

My hard body case is like a suit of armour.

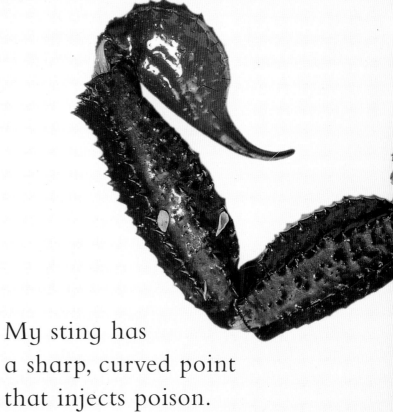

My sting has
a sharp, curved point
that injects poison.

I am about as long as an adult's hand.

I am a slimy banded snail.

I creep slowly along on my soft, squishy foot. I make a gooey trail of slime to help me slide along more easily.

My shell is a tube that coils round in a spiral. It grows as I do.

I carry my home on my back.

I scrape bits off plants
with rows of tiny teeth
on my tongue.
My tongue is called
a radula.

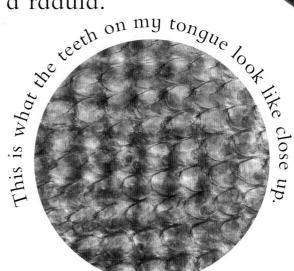

This is what the teeth on my tongue look like close up.

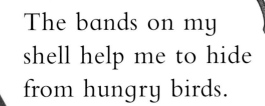

The bands on my
shell help me to hide
from hungry birds.

My eyes are at the tip
of my long feelers, called
tentacles. My short
tentacles help me
to smell things.

Important words

antenna A long thin stalk on an insect's head, used for detecting movement, smells and tastes.

nectar A sugary liquid made by flowers.

nymph A stage in the lifecycle of some insects, when they look like small adults without wings.

palp A short thick feeler near the mouth of spiders and insects.

pollen A yellow dust produced by flowers.

pupa The resting stage in the lifecycle of some insects, during which they turn into adults.

tentacle A long bendy structure like an arm, near an animal's mouth. It may have suckers or stings.

Index